FORESTS

By Melissa Cole

BLACKBIRCH®
PRESS

THOMSON
★
GALE

San Diego • Detroit • New York • San Francisco • Cleveland • New Haven, Conn. • Waterville, Maine • London • Munich

For more information, contact
The Gale Group, Inc.
27500 Drake Rd.
Farmington Hills, MI 48331-3535
Or you can visit our Internet site at http://www.gale.com

Photo Credits: Cover, all photos © Tom and Pat Leeson Wildlife Photography; pages 21, 25 illustrations by Chris Jouan Illustration

LIBRARY OF CONGRESS CATALOGING-IN-PUBLICATION DATA

Cole, Melissa S.
 Forests / by Melissa S. Cole.
   v. cm. — (Wild America habitats)
 Contents: Climate — Vegetation — Animals — Food — Humans and forests.
  ISBN 1-56711-802-X (hardback : alk. paper)
  1. Forest ecology—Juvenile literature. [1. Forests and forestry. 2. Forest ecology.
3. Ecology.] I. Title. II. Series: Wild America habitats series.

QH541.5.F6 C63 2003
577.3—dc21   2002012463

Printed in China
10 9 8 7 6 5 4 3 2 1

Contents

Introduction 4

Where Are Forests Found Today? 6

What Makes Forests Unique? 8

Types of Trees 10

Layers of Plants 12

How Do Animals Survive in Forests? 14

Food 16

Life in the Forest 18

Food Chain 20

Humans and Forests 22

A Forest's Food Web 23

Glossary 24

For Further Reading 24

Index 24

Introduction

Trees once covered more than half of North America. For centuries, humans have cut down many millions of trees for wood and to make room for agriculture. For the most part, trees have been cut down much faster than new ones can grow to replace them. That has caused forests—groups of trees in certain areas—to be on the decline for generations.

Forests are made up of large groups of trees that grow close together.

4

Forests are a special habitat, or type of environment where only certain plants and animals can survive. Scientists divide forest habitats into two major groups. They are coniferous forests and temperate deciduous forests. Coniferous forests are filled with evergreens and other trees that produce cones. These trees do well in cool climates.

Temperate deciduous trees have broad, flat leaves. These trees grow new leaves each spring. They also bear nuts and berries in summer, and shed their leaves in autumn. They remain bare throughout winter.

Pinecones (top) grow on trees in coniferous forests, while maple leaves grow on trees in temperate deciduous forests.

Where Are Forests Found Today?

Forests are found in many places in North America. Temperate deciduous forests grow where the climate offers warm summers and cold winters, such as in eastern North America. They also grow on the Great Plains in the west, and near the Great Lakes in the north.

Coniferous forests also grow in many places. Conifer trees are strong and can withstand severe weather conditions. Some conifers grow in northern places that have short summers and harsh, snowy winters. Other types of conifers grow in southern and southwestern parts of the United States. They do well in places with poor soil and minimal rainfall.

Evergreen trees can survive cold, snowy winters.

Sequoia National Park, California

Sequoia National Park is the second-oldest national park in the United States. It was established in 1890 to protect the big sequoia trees in the Giant Forest. The Giant Forest was named in 1875 by explorer and conservationist John Muir. He was amazed by the size of these evergreen trees, which are members of the redwood family.

Around 25 million years ago, sequoias grew all across North America. Over the last million years, though, the earth cooled, and most sequoias died. They are still found in California, west of the Sierra Nevadas. Sequoias grow in groups called groves. Only 75 groves still exist in an area 260 miles (418 km) long and 15 miles (24 km) wide.

Sequoias can grow to be more than 250 feet (76 m) tall with trunks more than 30 feet (9 m) wide. They can live for over 3,000 years!

General Sherman is the name given to one of the giant trees in Sequoia National Park. It is 274 feet (84 m) tall, and the trunk is 102 feet (31 m) around at the ground. It is probably more than 2,000 years old.

What Makes Forests Unique?

Each type of forest needs a certain kind of climate to exist. Conditions in different parts of North America allow for certain types of trees to grow. Generally, trees that grow farthest north are conifers. Conifers need at least 30 days each year when the daily average temperature is above 50°F (10°C) to grow.

In boreal or northern forests, winters are cold with some snowfall. Summers are warm and rainy. Boreal forests receive between 12 and 33 inches (30 and 84 cm) of rain each year. Average yearly temperature ranges from -65°F to 30°F (-54° to -1°C) in winter and 20°F to 70°F (-7° to 21°C) in summer.

Douglas fir and hemlock trees grow in a triangular shape, which lets snow slide off their branches.

Deciduous trees need three times as many warm days as conifers do to grow. The average yearly temperature in temperate deciduous forests is approximately 75°F (24°C). There is no true dry season. Rain falls throughout the year, averaging 30 to 80 inches (76 to 203 cm) annually.

Conifers are well adapted to cold weather. They have thin, wax-covered leaves called needles. Needles are thick and strong. They are able to retain water for long periods of time. Because they are so hardy, they continue to grow in winter. Conifer seeds are protected inside hard pinecones. These trees have a triangle shape. This allows snow to slide off easily without breaking branches. Lodgepole pines, black spruce, and sequoia trees often grow in dry, fire-prone areas. These trees have pinecones that open up after a fire and drop seeds in the ash. This reseeds the forest floor.

Conifer seeds grow inside hard pinecones. This protects them from being eaten by most animals.

Deciduous trees go through a special process each fall to get ready for winter when there is little water or sunlight. In spring and summer, leaves on deciduous trees produce and store food. These leaves have a chemical called chlorophyll that makes them green. Chlorophyll absorbs sunlight. Water, sunlight, and carbon dioxide (a gas) combine in a process called photosynthesis to form sugar in leaves. Sugar is food for trees. Trees must have plenty of sunlight to produce food. In winter, when days are shorter, there is not enough sunlight for leaves to absorb. Without sunlight, photosynthesis shuts down. Chlorophyll fades as the leaves stop producing sugar. In fall, trees feed off of food stored in the leaves. As leaves are drained of their sugar supply, they die. They turn from green to red and yellow. The tree becomes dormant, or inactive, until spring. During this time, the dead leaves fall off of diciduous trees. With spring comes longer days with plenty of sunshine. Once again, trees sprout leaves, and the process of making food through photosynthesis starts again.

Maple leaves turn from green to red and yellow as they die.

Layers of Plants

Trees share forests with many other plants. These plants live at various levels in the forest—in layers—and, together, form a forest habitat.

The top layer of a forest is called the canopy, or overstory. Here, only the highest trees get consistent sunlight. They create shade for everything below them. Small trees make up the second layer, called the understory. These trees live in the spaces where sun shines through the canopy. Low shrubs and bushes make up the next layer. They form a thicket. They usually grow no taller than 6 feet (1.8 m) high.

An herb layer of ferns, grasses, and wildflowers grows close to the forest floor. The ground layer is made up of mosses, liverworts, lichens, slime molds, and fungi.

The herb layer of a forest is made up of tall grasses and ferns.

Slime molds begin life as a single cell in the shady parts of the forest. Eventually, millions of these cells come together and form a slimy mass. It creeps along the forest floor and consumes pieces of rotten wood, decaying leaves, and small mushrooms. Flowering plants that live in the lower herb layer of the forest bloom and set seed in spring. This allows them to absorb as much sunlight as possible before the new leaves on broadleaf trees grow large and block out the sun.

Fungi sometimes grow along the trunks of rotting trees.

How Do Animals Survive in Forests?

Many predators, such as bobcats, foxes, and wolves, have thick coats to keep them warm in winter. Some animals, including lynxes, snowshoe hares, and wolverines, have broad, furry paws that spread their weight over a large area so that they do not sink in snow.

Voles, weasels, and snowshoe hares survive winter temperatures by making burrows. They dig down into the snow to keep warm. Just 10 inches (25 cm) under the snow, the temperature stays around 32°F (0°C). Animals' body heat warms up the burrow— and there is no wind to carry the heat away.

Some animals fall into a deep sleep during winter. This is called hibernation. During hibernation, an animal's heartbeat slows and its body temperature drops. It does not eat, drink, or produce waste while in this state. This saves energy and gives the animal a better chance of surviving until spring when rivers swell and food is abundant.

Beavers live along rivers. They chisel around the trunks of trees with their teeth. Once they have eaten away enough of the trunk, they topple it. They use these fallen trees to make log dams.

Beavers build dams with logs and sticks.

Alongside dams, beavers build a lodge of branches and mud. These structures can be up to 6 feet (1.8 m) tall. Beavers line the inner area of the shelter with wood shavings. This is where they sleep and raise their young.

Seventy percent of birds that live in the forest migrate to warmer climates to escape cold winter months. They fly as far south as South America. Once the temperature warms up, they return to their home in the forest.

Food

Forest habitats are filled with rich food sources that feed many animals. For example, flies and butterflies eat leaves. The larvae (caterpillars and grubs) of some moths, flies, and butterflies are flat enough to tunnel inside leaves. They are able to feed on the leaf without being spotted by predators. These bugs are called leaf miners. They are able to eat as much as they need to safely.

Caterpillars feed on leaves.

Grizzly bears can find food almost anywhere. They have long claws that allow them to scoop out the insides of rotten logs. Bears may eat some wood in the process, but they are looking to eat larvae and grubs (of beetles, moths, etc.). They can snag salmon from icy streams and dig up juicy lily bulbs from forest soil.

The red crossbill, a type of bird, feeds exclusively on pinecone seeds. This bird has a twisted beak that is used to pry open pinecones. A crossbill can poke its beak in between the cone scales. Then, it uses its tongue to remove seeds.

Nesting birds can live high in the canopy or lower in the understory. Some feed on seeds, while others prey on a plentiful supply of insects. Birds scatter seeds, berries, and cones. This helps trees to grow in new areas.

Top: Grizzly bears use their long claws to dig up roots to eat. **Bottom:** Crossbills only feed on pinecone seeds.

Life in the Forest

Forest habitats offer unique hiding places for both predators and prey. Owls are predators that live in the forest. They spend their days resting inside hollow trees. At night, they fly silently through the forest to look for small animals and insects to eat. Their huge eyes provide them with keen night vision—they can make out shapes in almost complete darkness. Owls can hear a mouse step on a leaf up to 75 feet (23 m) away!

Various types of small animals also inhabit forests. Squirrels and chipmunks run chattering along tree branches. They make their nests in trees out of leaves and branches. Mice, rabbits, and bats burrow underground or inside hollow trees. Raccoons spend their days sleeping in high tree branches. At night, they come down to fill their bellies with bird eggs, berries, and insects. Porcupines find shelter in trees or in hollow logs on the forest floor. They feed on tree bark and pine needles. Animals in the weasel family, such as pine martens, prey on mice, rabbits, bird eggs, and insects.

Sphinx moths blend in with the bark of trees.

Some animals are able to blend in with the environment. They are able to hide without moving from where they stand. Praying mantises, walking stick insects, and moths are shaped like leaves, twigs, and bark. These insects look like the forest vegetation and so predators may not notice them.

Certain species of flies, bees, beetles, and wasps dig into plants such as oak trees. This causes the plant to grow round bulbous knots called galls. Insects lay eggs inside galls and use them for protection. Baby bugs can munch on leaves that surround galls as soon as they hatch.

Owls have excellent vision that helps them hunt at night.

Plants and animals are connected to each other through the transfer of energy. For example, an evergreen tree uses energy in the form of sunlight to produce sugar. It stores sugar in its needles, roots, shoots, and cones. When a snowshoe hare eats pine needles, it gains energy from the sugar. When a lynx eats the hare, energy flows into the lynx. Scavengers, such as ravens and turkey vultures, eat a lynx after it dies and its energy transfers to them. Worms, bacteria, fungi, and insects—called decomposers—gain energy when they eat the rest of the animal. Any leftovers become part of the soil. When an evergreen tree absorbs leftover nutrients through its roots, the cycle begins all over again. As trees and other plants convert energy from sunlight to sugar, they release large quantities of oxygen into the air. Animals and people could not survive on earth without trees to create oxygen.

Lynxes and snowshoe hares are part of the food chain in a forest.

20

A Forest's Food Chain

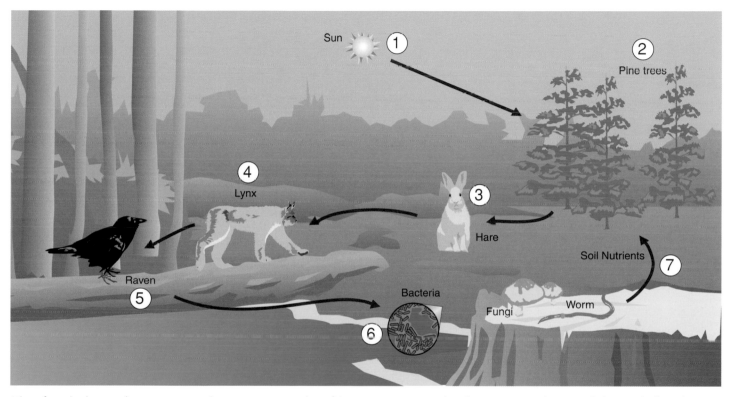

This food chain shows a step-by-step example of how energy in the forest is exchanged through food: The sun (1) is the first source of energy for all living things on earth. Green plants such as pine trees (2) are able to use sunlight and carbon dioxide in the air to create sugar, which the plants use as food. The pine trees' needles and cones are then eaten by the hare (3), which in turn is killed and eaten by the lynx (4). When the lynx dies, its flesh becomes food for ravens (5) and other scavengers. Worms, fungi, bacteria, and other decomposers (6) feed on the rest of the lynx's body. Finally, these creatures or their waste products end up as soil nutrients (7), which are then taken up by the roots of the pine trees as part of their nourishment. Then, the cycle starts again.

Humans and Forests

Native Americans lived in forests for thousands of years before European settlers arrived. Because Native Americans planted crops on small plots of land, they had very little impact on forests.

European settlers cut down more than 500 million acres of forest in just 100 years. They used logs to build houses and factories. They cleared forestland for agriculture.

When companies cut down whole forests for lumber or agriculture, it is called clear cutting. This causes the soil to erode, or wash away. That is because tree roots hold soil in place. When trees are uprooted, there is nothing to hold the soil. Eventually, the eroded area becomes barren.

One of the best ways for people to protect the forests is to buy recycled paper products. This helps to reduce the need for paper and saves trees. Using cloth napkins, bags, and diapers instead of paper ones is another way to reduce the need for paper. Forests can recover if people work hard to save them.

Humans have cut down millions of acres of forest to make room for communities.

A Forest's Food Web

A habitat's food web shows how all the creatures in the habitat depend on one another to survive. The arrows in this drawing show the flow of energy from one creature to another in the forest food web. The light yellow arrows point to those creatures nourished by the sun; namely, green plants such as trees, shrubs, and flowers. Green arrows point to the animals that eat the green plants for energy-mice, deer, squirrels, and so on. Dark yellow arrows move from these plant eaters to the predators that eat them. Finally, the dark red arrows show how the energy from the predators is used and released by scavengers like ravens and decomposers such as fungi and bacteria after the predators die. The energy returns to the soil and is taken up by green plants, and the cycle repeats. If any parts of this web disappear or weaken, the other parts are affected. If the trees are cut down, the beavers and squirrels disappear and so do their predators, and so on.

Glossary

Boreal Forest A northern forest containing mostly evergreen trees

Conifer A tree that has its seeds contained in pinecones instead of nuts or berries

Deciduous Trees that lose their leaves in the autumn

Decomposers Animals that eat dead tissue and return nutrients to the soil

Food Chain The process of energy passing between organisms as they feed upon one another.

Food Web A series of food chains that are linked together

Habitat The area in which a plant or animal naturally lives.

Predators Animals, such as cougars, that hunt other animals for food

Prey An animal killed and eaten by another animal

For Further Reading

Books

Mania, Cathy and Robert. *A Forest's Life*. New York: Grolier Publishing, 1997.

Martin, Patricia. *Woods and Forests*. New York: Grolier Publishing, 2000.

Sayre, April Pulley. *Temperate Deciduous Forest*. New York: Twenty-First Century Books, 1994.

Schwartz, David. *The Hidden Life of the Forest*. New York: Crown Publishing, 1988.

Web sites

Sequoia National Forest page
http://www.r5.fs.fed.us/sequoia/

Sierra Club's boreal forest site
http://www.sierraclub.org/ecoregions/boreal.asp

Fun Facts about temperate deciduous forests
http://www.mbgnet.mobot.org/sets/temp/

Index

Beavers, 14-15
Boreal forests, 6, 8

Canopy, 12
Climate, 8-9
Coniferous forests, 5

European settlers, 22
Evergreen trees, 5, 6

Galls, 19

Hibernation, 14

Layers, 12
Leaves, changing, 11
Lodgepole pines, 10
Lynx, 20

Needles, 10, 18, 20

Owls, 18-19

Sequoia National Park, 7

Soil erosion, 22

Temperate deciduous forests, 5, 6

Thicket, 12

Understory, 12

p2/20   05/04

The Bryant Library
Roslyn, New York
(516) 621-2240